Nighthawk
Storyteller

Earth, water,
sun and sky —
Celebrate
them all !

DiAnne
Korda

Also by DyAnne Korda

The Shore's Absolute Edge
This Earth Woman
Finding the Lost Woman: A Poet's Journal

Nighthawk Storyteller

DyAnne Korda

dyannekorda.com

With deep gratitude to:

Scott Stowell, Donna Decker,
Amy Dosser, Gloria Zager
and Mustang Sally

Special thanks to:

Michael Goldberg of KAXE/KBXE Northern Community Radio
Agates, the League of Minnesota Poets' journal
The H&D Harbor Poets

This publication is made possible in part by
the voters of Minnesota through a grant from
the Arrowhead Regional Arts Council
thanks to a legislative appropriation from
the Arts and Cultural Heritage Fund.

Cover art: Meinrad Craighead, *Nighthawk Storyteller*, 1986

ISBN: 979-8-218-71961-6

Ely, Minnesota
2025

For
Meinrad Craighead
N. Scott Momaday
Bear and Coyote

Contents

The place of infinite possibility is where
the storyteller belongs.

—N. Scott Momaday
The Man Made of Words

*****

So in their night flights, going home,
the poets sing and the storytellers speak and
the artists make pictures about the Riddle of Eternity.
The riddle unwinds as a journey
from the source back to the source.

The mystery of the riddle is the eternal cycle,
beginning and ending at the center in the entwined fingers.
I set upon this journey as an artist
from the laps of my ancestors...

—Meinrad Craighead
The Litany of the Great River

Nighthawk Storyteller
for Amy Dosser

They return in half-dim light like ribbons of river water
flowing above treetops.
A hundred soaring specks take shape—
feathers flashing white patches. They swing
graceful loops over the house as I catch my breath.

I know them well. On these summer nights, I can hear
once-upon-a-time tales of magical birds that make
no nests for precious eggs—so perfectly do they blend
with field and wood, their bodies vanish as they land.

I can see storytelling mothers
enfolding spellbound daughters in marvelous yarns
that mirror these birds' lightning sharp calls
as they sail through riddles of eternity.
Yes. Words from ancestors arrive on nighthawk wings.

What We Must Do

Lupin dreams on the bed; our husky
is swimming beyond faint veils,
finding her way back to my ancestors.

I haven't started laundry or dusted.
Instead, I've read awful news and
visited the Lake on YouTube; thankfully
she is swaying, her waves shining-alive.

I walk room to room,
searching for possessions to give away.
Cold weather clicks on the furnace;
birdsong is muted.

Apparitions of journal pages
float like delicate seed puffs.
We are made of words, Momaday says.

I am writing and Lupin
prepares to cross over.
Bless this broken world.
I am ready to be a poet again.

Hiddenness

When our town overflows with tourists
cavorting along snow-laced trails,
a neighbor playfully texts,

        Are you hiding?
Not in the way she assumes.

Imagining moist underground dens
where wild mothers burrow alone
to birth naked cubs,
        I wait inside bedroom walls
that often welcome the Northern Lights

    as shimmering poems
begin to emerge from prisms of stillness.

Winter Jar
for Emily Dickinson

Snow refuses to leave the pewter sky. Wind gathers,
tumbling flurries—steeps of frozen mounds for miles.
On the storm's third morning, I remember your birthday
while pouring mint tea. Beyond the kitchen clutter,
I see a clean mason jar that simply appears too empty.
After shoulder-pushing open the front door, there's a
sleigh-like drift cloaking bushes of wild roses.
I scoop and mash ivory crystals into the clear glass,
clumps of ice flakes slide over cold stiffening fingers.
This jar will stay on the shelf that holds your poems,
becoming pure water, waiting to nourish sunflower
seedlings that, come summer, will rise strong
from tended black earth.

From the Other Side

In the earliest moments
of morning darkness,

I awaken as the mattress
creaks with weight
from a jump on the bed.

Lupin circles twice then
lies down hard with a usual sigh.

Her astral body presses against
my blanketed feet. As always,
her simple canine touch

sends me back
to sleep.

Dreaming of Catherine
for my grandmother

While you and I stroll the garden,
wavering plants inhale sunlight.
We listen as roots stretch down,
winding around buried stones and we
leisurely gesture with our hands
at the symmetries and scents
of green abundance.

In the long fragrance of fresh blossoms,
      time pauses and
you wear a magnificent cape,
dark maroon with pale yellow fringe.
          Our eyes meet
and you nod. *Mourning cloak butterflies.*
Myriads of wings open and
close...

How to Fill Long Nights

Remember this black-feathered bird
whose purple beak
carries winter solstice prayers
of bread, candle and song.

Listen to this old woman
who speaks of frozen crystals
reeling from skies bruised with wind;
her stories begin thousands of years
before *frost* accepted its name.

Remember mythical beasts crawling in
from four directions of your childhood
to steal comfort through hibernation,
to renew hope through your innocent love
of all that is unknown.

New Year Ritual

I take the wooden broom with straw bristles
while listening to a recording of Lakeshore waves
rattling pebbles over sand. And I match
the grand rhythm, sweeping from one room to another.

Sprinkling dried croneswort in the abalone shell,
I pause before a picture of the Black Madonna,
Our Lady of Częstochowa, a sacred picture
handed down from grandmother to grandmother.

Now they stand with me—shoulder to shoulder
in pastel house dresses, thick sweaters
with patches, some wearing babushkas.

In every doorway, we smudge the herb
of *moon-dream wisdom.* Waves of smoke
sway above my writing desk,
books, our bed and makeshift altars.

When it's finished and only the watery music
of swirling stones remains, I sit down to eat
a slice of toast. The coffee tastes sweet and strong.

Blue Morning Light

The garden holds me
in a burgeoning web of birdsong.
From all directions, flute sounds rise.

> *Here*
Here
> > *Here*

Mist dissipates.   Near the maple's hunched roots,
Aunt Rose stands, olive shawl loose
under plump shoulders,   peasant skirt fluttering.

The grand tree rustles as Hannah descends.
My radiant sister, barefoot, laughing, branch-tousled hair,
her white sundress smudged leaf green.

> *Here*
Here
> > *Here*

The unmistakable howl; sled-dog legs kick up alley dust.
Lupin returns home to meet the puppy that arrived
ten days after she departed.

The garden breathes
rhythmic blue light; holding hands,
my family and I begin the ancient dance.

> *Here*
Here
> > *Here*

Floating

Brightness drifts from my blessing bowl.
Inside, amber flecks settle between teardrop seeds.
As the sun lifts above the lake, canine silhouettes
race in flickering grasses. Lupin and a rowdy pup.

Aunt Rose appears in a mauve robe with a moon medallion.
Sweeping the breeze with her chubby arms, she removes
the necklace, placing it upon my chest. And *snap*,
we are standing hip deep in the almost-frozen lake.
She sing-speaks the old language then dunks me down.

My eyes open with a frog's glistening view
of lily pads; rising echoes of my breath-bubbles
become Lupin's music to paddle circles around us.
With a loose grip, Rose twirls my body. Kicking up
muck, I break the horizon into light.

When Rose lifts me up, Lupin instantly swims
to shore, shaking her heavy coat to resume happy play.
With my aunt's gifted hands beneath my back,
I am floating, memorizing the morning sky.

Mustang Sally

In her avid puppy mind,
Sally believes that she's
the unbroken mustang,
galloping loopy figure-eights
in shabby backyard grass.
With eyes ablaze,
our flourishing husky
kicks and stomps.
Her unforgivable leash—
its tip clenched
in the middle
of a fierce little grin,
twirling behind.

The Dawning

Unfinished woman,
you've been wandering
along so many pathways
in folktale lands. From
forest to castle, you listen
as voices purl around you
with their separate lives and
long shadows of strange lyrics.

Woman, it's time
to stop at the crossroad
of Permanence and Change.
Punch the sky and wait.
With no umbrella,
you will have a clear view
to find that you are
standing at creation's dawn.

Early Summer

Bees crisscross
fresh blooms,
testing sweetness
and the puppy lies
on her wriggling
back, sun-kissed
belly up, forelegs
floppily waving—
directing
a silent
symphony.
She rolls
and sighs,
fur sprinkled
with whirlybird
maple seeds.

Slow Motion Love Poem

I
Because you named her Mustang Sally,
we open the car door and scoop her
into the puppy crate. It's just past sunrise
and time to *ride, Sally, ride.*
You grab a Pepsi; I take black coffee.

With one hour before her appointment
to be spayed, we must keep breakfast kibble
off her mind, so the three of us begin to drive
around the biggest, nearest body of water,
Shagawa Lake.

Without radio voices warning of COVID,
or classical music and membership drives,
the pacified puppy's eyes flutter and close
while the motor hums along.

We see waves of starlings migrating south
above yellow-red fields when you whisper,
*A nice six-point buck usually crosses
the road here. Yeah.   That's him.*

II
Pandemic protocol dictates we meet in the parking lot.
The young surgeon's hands reach for Sally's leash.
Her reassuring voice recites procedural information.
*Here is a copy of post-care instructions... Remember,
no news is good news... Do you have any questions?*

III
Sally naps comfortably on the kitchen rug.
Her recovery cone collar, black and
pink camouflage, is propped
on the table beside a bowl of bananas.

I've studied these healing instructions
until my thoughts tangle. *Keep puppy calm
for seven to ten days...* Mustang Sally?
And if she can't swim or bathe, can she lie in snow?

Heavy winds roll and tap at every window.
I don't want Sally out there,
leaping after twirling-down leaves
like a Sufi dervish seeking perfection.

Twenty-four hours have passed and not once
has she jumped or nipped or licked her incision.

I write, sitting on the floor near her. Clock ticking.
Clothes dryer spinning. Pen scratching over paper.

When I begin to read aloud, Sally looks up.
Touching her tongue to my lips,
she tastes words from the first poem
that belongs only to her.

When I Feel Lost

Muted sun through damp air will fuel thunderstorms.
Grand as they are, sunflowers are bowing
as bees feast in flowering centers.
So far, a minimal garden. Did the seeds know
my heart wasn't present when I planted them?

Soaring through star clusters, somewhere
between the living and dead, my thoughts escaped.
But now they're hovering like hummingbirds
descending from slender branches to the feeder
with fresh sugar water. I remember

as a child, learning to feel comfortable
with mystery, walking my auntie's yard
faithfully with watering cans overflowing,
soaking her sunlit marigolds.

And even now, the old cookpot rattles
with blood-red water as beets come to boil;
close to the scent of vetiver—
Dark Mother, heart-soothing Earth.

She Echoes Thunder

When a lingering storm
ends, the Lake glows;
I toss her handfuls
of freshly-cut herbs.
As she echoes thunder
and whispers prayers to Mary,
her ravenous waves swallow
my gift of chamomile,
lavender and thyme.
With one swoosh,
the satisfied crone
pulls me down
until pearly bubbles
surge from my lips
and I dive for
the brightest
stone below.

The Arrival

The hand-me-down happy-birthday box
has a dented cardboard cover
      wrapped with faded paper
of neon blue cartoon crocodiles on parade—
      tinka-tinka-tinking tambourines,
oom-pa-paing saxophones,
      bang-crashing bongos and
            pluck-picking jazzy guitars.
Their toothy mouths
belting out *tra-la-la-boom-dee-ay.*

So I'm not surprised
that when I reach for the box,
      it begins to rattle and
a pointy canine muzzle
      jostles free the lid.

      Yellow eyes blink and
one lean brush wolf rises up—
stretching slow and yoga-like.
      Strawberry blond
with grizzled buff.   Red legs
      and a bushy, black-tipped tail.
      Enter Coyote.

Tricksters Are Known

Coyote scratches his neck with his back foot
then circles the mattress for a mid-morning wink
while I try out my new tarot deck.

                                Flipping cards from
side to side, I'm breathing to the rhythm
of Coyote's rolling snores. And

the final message makes no sense.
PAST: *Splendor and divinity.* PRESENT:
Examining identity. FUTURE: *Living in the dark.*

              Damn.
If that's where I'm heading,
          then where have I been?

As Coyote trots through deep-forest dreams,
         I pace the hallway—
bedroom to living room,

circling back to the bathroom mirror
          and noting that muddy confusion
is dulling my eyes.   Then it hits me.

Tricksters are known   to operate in reverse.
Still asleep, Coyote's whiskers twitch; his lips
purse into a beaming grin.

         I touch his pointed nose
and ebony-tipped tail—receiving a jolt—
his indestructible creative disorder.

Almost-Poem

Words swim in fruitful silence,
mixing metaphors like potions.
They shout and splash
in my deep-night brain
simply demanding poetry.
With a pen on the bedstand,
my palm serves as paper
since I'm forced to write
in darkness. Come
morning, I'm careful not
to wash this almost-poem
down the shower drain
because all day at my day job,
these words will keep
faithful company
as they show me the way.

Witness

Mustang Sally is somewhere in the house.
I find her—tail thwacking on the edge of the bed.
She's listening intently to a photograph of Rose.
Fading black and white, I can't see my aunt's lips move
but Sally tilts her head this way and that, as Rose tells stories
about me. She's aware that I'm drawn to forests and dogs,
gardens with beets and sunflowers.
In my post-menopausal body, Rose recognizes
women who were missing from our family branches.
Rose understands why I believe that all lakes
and God's Mother have something in common.
She knows why I see mournful faces
in certain stones; why I feed braided herbs to fire.
And yes, as a husky pup, Sally must feel this way, too—
the moon has always pulled us in particular ways;
that's why Rose and I meet often in waking dreams.
Mustang Sally stands on the mattress and reaches
her front paws to the windowsill. Nose to glass,
she's determined to witness twilight.

Amulet Ceremony

In bowing grasses, Hannah and I sit among dragonflies.
She playfully wraps Aunt Rose's babushka over
my squinting eyes as sunlight presses upon the lake.

Blindfolded, I hear the old women shuffling
through the overgrown field; they breathe in unison—
a deep, slow rhythm.

With tenderness, Hannah turns my palms up—as I sense
the steady flow of grandmothers dropping seeds, and
placing damp stones with bits of weeds in my open hands.

When she unties the floral scarf, we are alone
except for a Tawny Owl with Rose's flashing eyes—
perched on a pine branch, talons clutching a weathered bone.

Shadow

As the
settling
sun
strokes
the narrow
arched
back
of this
leafless
white
birch
I raise
my autumn
eyes
and she
casts
her grateful
shadow
upon
my face

Bear Feast

Before the holiday became Halloween, it was called *Dziady* in Poland—when the veil between our world and the spirit world seems thinnest. It is the day I awaken sometime around 6 a.m. The kitchen nightlight glows soft ivory. I pour enough coffee grounds for four cups, flick on the coffeemaker then whip my beloved blanket over my shoulders. It's one for shaking away chill—made from good wool with a colorful bear mask design called *She Who Watches*. Chickadees, evening grosbeaks and downy woodpeckers weave to and fro from our window feeder to various tree branches rising above the river flowing north.

When Scott finishes his journal writing, we move around the kitchen with minimal words as if our dance was carefully choreographed. I rinse and slice carrots, celery, potatoes, and chop onions while he tends to the plum-colored meat. "Smell the freshness," Scott invites. I do. The meat smells venison-like. Wild. He scoops up remaining fat, opens the back door and tosses it to the grass, an offering for whiskey jacks and woodpeckers. I add sugar, tapioca, tomatoes, breadcrumbs, garlic, oregano and Worcestershire sauce. We pour the combined ingredients into the crock and turn the dial on low.

This morning is grey mist with the scent of fallen leaves and winding roads. We drive several miles to the grocery store as the wild rice calls for green onions and red peppers. We already bought the wine, Syrah, a California brand called *Barefoot*. This bottle is a roundabout way of acknowledging the beginning. My tattoo, bear footprints, has circled my ankle for a few years. That act, before I met bears, marked my devotion to them.

Early afternoon, Scott drives to the Echo Trail. He's searching for the right place to hunt deer this season. Our house trailer is silent; I pick up my wooden flute. Slow, low notes gather and give way to an improvisational melody that appears bittersweet but matter-of-fact. As bear association directors, Scott and I took risks and worked ourselves flat-out through nauseating exhaustion with disapproving results. Sanctuary people did not understand. Bear Spirit did. We gave ourselves; she ate us. Tonight we celebrate Dziady with bear meat stew. Tonight Bear and I shall become each other.

Holding the flute in my lap, I close my eyes and concentrate. Once my breath smooths over, a waking dream presents itself. I am seated in matted grasses deep in trees. A bear den is to my front and left, dug inside a ridge. She is in there— raking, fluffing, shaping those pine-speckled grasses into a bed. I will sit with the *She Who Watches* blanket draped over my shoulders—to be with her as she nods herself to sleep. And I will come daily when the sun's low angle highlights spinning crystals that will settle upon the den creating a blue snowy mound. To be near her in crisp silence.

After meditating, my knee-high rubber boots, still muddy from early-morning feedings at the bear sanctuary, take me down the wet, dirt road. It winds away from our trailer through woods dotted with vacant summer cabins. A weighty pine aroma wraps around my raincoat. I wear the hood—and with every uphill step, my echoing breath remains even.

When Scott returns home from scouting the forest, we chop and sauté vegetables, then allow the rice to simmer. We position our chairs near our favorite window and the river below shines with hardly a ripple. Finches and jays flit to the food tray; they crack open sunflower seeds. Hairy woodpeckers nibble suet. Earlier I found a piece of writing to set our ceremony in motion. I hand Scott *In the Bear's House*, a collection by N. Scott Momaday, and point to "The Khanty Bear Feast," a poem in the voice of the dead bear who's about to be eaten. When I ask him to read aloud, Scott hesitates for half a second only, then does so with care.

We pop open beers as the sun drops into the forest past the river. And music. Clint Black reminds us that autumn brings a change in the air. Lucinda Williams affirms the raw emotions of leaving and letting go. Lyle Lovett sings, *They just don't come no better than a bear*. Scott and I discuss winter and rest and the unknown. We shall greet spring with a solid plan to move our lives along.

The sweet fragrance of stew and the earthy scent of rice carry a message. Our meal is ready. We arrange our fine silverware with the bear footprint designs, delicate wine glasses (an engagement present from Scott's parents), and department store plates. I dip the serving spoon into the glass casserole, create a bed of wild rice then ladle the dark rich stew, covering the rice.

I choose music played by a gifted violinist, Eli Bissonett, to accompany our feast. "Pachelbel Canon in D" floats through the room as Scott pours the deep purple wine, smelling of lavender. We toast to Bear Spirit. To us. To our future together. I taste, allowing the first morsel of meat to almost-melt on my tongue. Bear's tender warmth fills me.

Midwinter

Listen.
Beneath
cold silence,
another
kind of place.

Bare maple
branches;
one cedar
waxwing trills
sighing
whistles.

Her beak,
a crescent
shadow; her
eyes brimming
with sunlight.

Beneath White Branches

Wind rattles paper bark on this tree
near my bedroom window.
Dried leaves already tossed down,

only an ensnared feather
twirls madly on the tip
of a random branch.

For seven months, I've paused daily
to watch the thinning feather,
a tiny lock of Babusia's hair,

clinging to its place
on a wispy limb—
even as blizzards churn.

But this morning, winter
becomes spring
and the feather is missing.

Now I see that it rests
in Babusia's furrowed hand.
She stands beneath white branches

and nods to a threadbare book
of Dickinson poems
propped upon clawed roots —

her grin, displaying
a single tooth,
promises *Hope.*

The Bears Keep Pace

Mist glides through the meadow as bears awaken.
Bellies drumming with hunger, their grand silhouettes
pad through frosty mud in procession as if they
are praying their way through worn labyrinths.

In the middle of the field, Rose and Babusia
wear their wool sweaters over everyday dresses;
they sit at a folding table with three mismatched cups,
a stoneware pitcher, and fresh deck of cards.
I wonder if they plan to read tarot or play pinochle.

Rose calls to me as Babusia cuts the deck.
I sit on the available tree stump stool tucked under
the table; Babusia slides me paper and pen.
As Rose pours the honey mead, my cup shudders,
then doubles its size. Within steam rising from
the rim, luminous words waver.

Babusia winks in affirmation when I reach
for her writing pad and raise the cup to my lips.
Crisp air holds a blossoming sweetness;
catkins dangle from aspen tips.
Around us, the silent bears keep pace,
weaving through grassland haze.

Close to Midnight

I hold a singing bowl and face the Lake.
Rose comes with the moon following,
its high glow flickers upon
her shawl's feathered edge.

Rose smiles. Standing before me,
her eyes rest upon the copper basin.
So close—yet without a touch—her hands
sweep circles above the bowl; it resonates

absolute pitch. The moon's reflection tumbles inside,
prompting countless stars to spill skyward.
They burst in flashing canopies and
capture this dreamless night, like
spiderwebs drenched in dew.

First Day of Spring

After driving around knee-high snowbanks
for the better half of the morning, searching for
genuine greenness in flower and seed stores—
passing up snake plants, cactus, philodendrons,
and choosing a violet with purple-fringed blooms—

Mustang Sally and I head for pine-filled trails.
When we slip into the woods, doubt ransacks
my new Coyote poems. Only three—yet

they seem way too similar—especially the bits
about the tip of his tail. Should I revise?
Will more come? Am I done? At least for now?

Along the bending route, he simply appears—
white teeth, panting tongue, adolescent legs, racing
directly at us. Ten feet to spare, Coyote looks up, then
veers left in thickets along the cedar grove and vanishes.

I'm uncertain why
I wasn't surprised at Sally's nonreaction—
then notice her snowy tracks perfectly match his.

On the path, there's a fawn's joint-bone
gnawed to the nub—and as I reach, a familiar voice
whispers, *You want poems? Take it.*

When I Finally Understand Mustang Sally Has Been My Muse All the While

Sally studies the steam rising from my tea cup
while she learns to be my creative muse.
We sit on the bed together; the heat kicks on.
Dust specks float past her nose and she snaps
to catch them, hoping for mosquito meat.
She chews her toenails, gnaws on a deer tine,
bites my sleeve as my hand takes pen
across this tattered journal page.

Rolling to her belly, Sally places her chin
on my shins, her legs flat on a forty-year-old
Pendleton Blanket—which she nips, like
the ornery fabled dragon, piercing wool
with her almost two-year-old teeth. I scold,
Where's your bone? Her brown eyes spark and
ears point forward. She jauntily tilts her head.
I have more than one. Which do you mean?

Sunlight and silence make my thoughts fertile.
For the third time, Sally dozes and runs
through stormy fantasies until I decide to follow.
She travels the edges, where paths meet woods,
where rivers meet loam. Her heartbeat echoes

old-woman stories of invisible edges, thin red lines
that divide Ordinary from Mystical. Over and over,
I write certain phrases, slightly altering them until
they appear like magical chants hidden on paper.
Sally sleeps. Her front paw rests upon my ankle.

Oneness

Her license plate reads "Oneness."
The woman has driven long miles to the Lake.
Arriving before sunrise, she unloads canvas bags
filled with kindling, a writing journal,
snacks, a good bottle of wine,
hand drums and her husband's ashes.

The woman wears tie-dye—
a fiery crimson sweatshirt
over a flowing copper-blue dress.
In her stone circle on the shore, flames
shimmer around passing seagull shadows.

Wild gusts ruffle her hair.
Bushes filled with rose hips
cast off shriveled leaves;
they tumble between the pages
of her open journal lying on sand.

When the woman's song is finished,
she notices her grandmother's ghost
hanging white pillowcases and
sheets with wooden clothespins
above the shore's edge.

Near her grandmother's feet,
the woman sees a lucent pebble,
like an egg, resting on the beach.
Slowly, her intimate sorrow
drifts free as she warms the stone
in the center of her hand.

Her Own Lush Dreams

In my neighbors' garden, I'm invited
to pick ripe blueberries,
nettles and tender buds of garlic.
With a thermos of lemon balm tea,
I sit near overflowing borage
to admire countless bumblebees.
Green stems stir with hovering flight
and gathering pollen, while the bees hum
wandering songs from not-so-distant fairylands.
Their splendid queen naps on a sturdy leaf
and I touch her fuzzy roundness with my finger tip.
She turns her sweet head, antennas slightly twitch
before reentering her own lush dreams.

Goddess of Protection

Long ago on any windy day, if you'd ask me
to be the hundred-pound anchor of flesh and bone
by moving to the front of our flat-bottom boat
to weigh down unruly waves bouncing the prow,
I may have taken offense. Yet today I choose
to become our fishing boat's living figurehead.
As Goddess of Protection, I'm perched upon
the front aluminum seat, lake-splashed torso
pitched forward, taming the reckless storm—
as you steer us gingerly to shoreline silt
near the tall leaning tree where a
red-winged black bird sings
to lost fishing lures, tangled
in sunbeams on a branch below.

Coyote Roams My House

until the moon appears.
Stomach grumbling, he sniffs something good
tucked in the basement.
He zeros in on a cardboard box
stuffed with newspapers that he tosses
until he's juggling the prize—six green tomatoes—
upstairs to the kitchen.
Pulling drawers and slamming cupboards,
he searches for spatulas and pans.
Coyote plans to sling the tart fruit
with gloopy eggs.
But first he shuffles through music looking for
that solid rock groove—like Tom Petty,
Patti Smith or Beck.
Yipping along, he chops and stirs
as tunes boom. Toenails click-tap
around the stove. Grub dripping down his chin,
Coyote smacks his lips,
chewing to the beat until his belly
won't hold another tidbit.
So he teeters upon my tall bookshelf
to skim *The Tao of Pooh*
and snooze the afternoon away.

Amber Rosary

My first rosary in fifty years,
honey-colored amber,
fossilized sap said to bring
sweetness, peace.

Almost before time,
these wild old pines
thrived near Babusia's
home on the rolling edge
of water and earth,

where she would sit
with the breath of sky
and natural melodies
of resin-blood simmering
beneath furrowed bark

into this string
of prayers.
Cross and beads,
warm to touch.

A Kind of Magic

In Ketchum, Idaho,
  a ladder leads down
to a windowless basement,

where inside a dark closet-sized tent,
  hanging lights showcase
trays of white bell-shaped flowers.

Firefly petunias
  generate their own light.
Scientists are celebrating

the combination of
  a cultivated plant's metabolic cycle
with a bioluminescent mushroom

*to bring a kind of magic
into our lives.*
                    Stop.

Somehow, you must recall
  lying in that vacant lot near
your first home—a wavering field

of wild hawkweed, clover and bees.
You listened intently with your eyes
  emanating stars.

    Of course,
your mother's petunias glowed.

Quiet Pond

There is seldom the slightest ripple on Quiet Pond,
a little round lake cupped in steep woodland banks.
But this morning, Mustang Sally and I witness
upon the water, glistening oval loops spooling out
from a soaked furry face. Pit Bull? Bear cub?

Sally and I creep closer, remaining inconspicuous
behind *this* wide trunk—or *that* tall stump—and
sploosh! A hidden flat tail smacks the hazy surface.

When surprise fades to familiar stillness,
Sally sits; her tail thumps earth and her eyes
widen into *wasn't that fascinating?*

Our shared reveries vanish
once a walker appears—chugging along.
Snug earbuds tucked in place beneath a Nike cap,
her Pegasus Blueprint sneakers tap with
the heated beat of political podcast brawls.

She keeps walking—without turning back—
as I holler through laughter, "Did you see the beaver's
grand pronouncement!"   Nor does she notice the raven;

black feathers puffed, body rocking the branch above.
Gurgling croaks, shrill screeches, raspy caws—
a long litany of everything that's sacred here.

To Receive Wisdom

One silver hair lies on my pillowcase
and I suddenly think of Georgia O'Keeffe. Her
face, intricate and beautiful—like cedar trees.

I study her watercolor ways. How she wraps
evening-star hues around smooth rocks, jack-
in-the-pulpits and open clam shells—

even a blackbird with snowy
red hills. Miss O'Keeffe's humor
matches the landscape of adobe and bone.

Flicking bits of dog crackers off my bed,
I picture her beloved chows, Bo and Chia,
following intently as she walks purple earth
with her wooden cane in low sun.

And I place my own silver strand
in the blessing bowl—soon, a gift
for the waning moon.

Keeper of the Dreams

Who can argue with the wisdom of a child
who has known too much. A girl who
hopscotches around locked doll houses
that hoard top-shelf dreams.

Here is the child who will see
widows' faces from beyond the grave
in wildflowers and fresh snow.
She will sense the aloneness
of their extinguished worlds

spinning with fog in silent forests
because their desperate faith
has infused fallen leaves with rocks—
lasting adornments in this timebound place.

Before Leaving, I Try to Memorize the Lake

when Crow alights on the dead, standing aspen,
a thick pillar positioned midway
among healthy shoreline trees.

        She surveys the Lake slowly
and finally, the shining pearl within her eye
rests upon my face.
          I somehow understand
that Crow has agreed
to lead this morning meditation.

        We regard the Lake
together, with our own
Buddhist hand bells—bronze churning waves.
          She stays

until I return to myself,
      remembering home,
not far from here.   In this moment,
Crow rises, hovers and departs.

        At the shoreline,
I pocket a black, oval pebble.   Cold water
spills freely through my cradling hands.

Solstice Campfire

Morning light begins to flicker through snowing skies.
Pajamas, thick socks and uncombed hair, I sit with our pup
near the holiday tree. Her elk tine gift rests at my feet.

She's finally about to doze and we are drenched
in her spit. Scattered antler shavings lie on my lap,
her arms, and what remains of this couch. Cinnamon
in my coffee and the furnace plinks like waterdrops

in the underground cavern of my imagination.
It's where all my aunties greet me. Hair adorned in flowers
and feathers. Dresses embellished with embroidery
and beading—poppies, hearts, keys and morning stars.

Within limestone walls carved smooth, their solstice
campfire gleams with potent ballads of Baba Yaga.
Dark and hopeful, this pregnant cave holds secrets.

Winter's Mother

Old Woman
sits on
a stump
of rusty oak
Leathered bare
foot bottoms
pressed
Her curved
toes touch

Old Woman
loves her
own body
new moon
eyes
and driftwood
arms folded
with craggy root
fingers locked
under her
muddy
chin

On raven
feathered nights
Old Woman
whispers
violet snow
then traces
She-bear's
meandering
dreams along
the boundless rim
of this hollow
sky

DyAnne Korda's previous books include *The Shore's Absolute Edge, This Earth Woman* and *Finding the Lost Woman: A Poet's Journal.*

She also teaches a variety of writing workshops and presents poetry readings that emphasize elements of oral storytelling traditions through written poetry. Her work reflects reverence for the natural world and illustrates how archetypal dreams can awaken a reality beyond the ordinary. By paying close attention to every season, Korda uses her experiences to help people understand their own connection to Earth.

She lives with her husband, Scott Stowell, and their Alaskan husky, Mustang Sally, in Ely, Minnesota.